# THE FLYING PINTO'S
# Flight Attendant
# Survival Guide

Written by Sara Keagle & Illustrated by Kelly Kincaid

# The Flying Pinto's

# Flight Attendant Survival Guide

# ACKNOWLEDGMENTS

This book was a true labor of love as this career has given me so much. I truly want to share my knowledge with those just beginning their flight attendant adventure. I'd like to thank Jennifer McDonnell for her help in editing, Kelly Kincaid for her beautiful art that added so much to the book, my galley gab friends that contributed laughter and advice and of course my family and friends for their amazing support.

# Prepare for Take Off
## A guide for surviving your first year as a flight attendant

*I boarded the plane that would take me on my new adventure! Grinning ear to ear as I felt this opportunity to attend flight attendant training would change the trajectory of my life. I headed down the aisle to find my seat assignment, there were already two other flight attendant candidates in my row. I sat in the aisle seat and we introduced ourselves. A few moments later the girl at the window leaned over and asked, "are you guys worried about the weight requirement?...well, I know you're not", she said to the girl in the middle....only to lean over closer to me and touch my knee, "are you?" She became my roommate for the next six weeks.*

Congratulations! Your life is about to change in a big way. The possibilities are now endless, the entire world just opened up to you. Not only because you will have flight benefits, but also because you will be exposed to many people and cultures and I'm just talking about on the flights you will be working! With this lifestyle however comes adjustments and my hope is that this guide will help you with everything you need to know to help you not only survive, but thrive in your first few years as a flight attendant. This career choice is not for everyone; a good number of you will find that out and quit within your first year…and that's OK. The experience you'll gain will be priceless. I have kept in touch with many people who quit within the first year of graduation from training and I don't know one who isn't happy that they had the experience. Many of them even wish they had stayed, so hopefully this guide will help those who should stay make it through the transitional first few years.

My wish for this guide is that it will help you navigate through the upcoming changes in your life, like where to live, how to pack, staying healthy, space available travel, how your friends and family may react to your new life, information on hotels and more.

One of the best things about becoming a flight attendant is your new flight attendant family. You will find a bond amongst your fellow trainees that will last a lifetime and you will suddenly have friends all over the world! Can you imagine running into a friend in Rome, Paris or even the airport in Detroit for that matter? This will happen all the time! Flight Attendants have the best tricks for just about anything and know the best places to eat at airports so be sure to ask them, they are a great resource for you. Remember to lean on your new colleagues too when you have questions or you just feel lonely; most likely they have felt the same way as you and have been through many of the same things. You are not alone on this new adventure!

Welcome on board!

# Family and Friends and Dating

*"Traveling is a brutality. It forces you to trust strangers and to lose sight of all that familiar comfort of home and friends. You are constantly off balance. Nothing is yours except the essential things-air, sleep, dreams, the sea, the sky-all things tending towards the eternal or what we imagine of it."*
-*Cesare Pavese*

*My boyfriend took me to the airport so I could fly off and attend flight attendant training at my new airline. We had both been so excited up to this point that we really hadn't thought about what this new career could mean for our relationship. As we looked at each other to say goodbye, I think reality finally set in that this wasn't a temporary goodbye. There was something very telling in his eyes. I found out much later that in that moment he knew he had lost me.*

When you found out you were accepted into flight attendant training everyone was so happy for you. In fact they were probably as ecstatic as you were. They may have even felt as though they won the lottery…after all, they're going to travel for free or close to it right? When you left for training everyone was probably a little sad, but still excited for this new adventure. Now you're on line and things may not be going so well for your loved ones. They miss you. You have already been gone for many weeks for flight attendant training and nobody realized you'd only have a quick trip home before heading off to your new base. Their world has also been turned upside down only they're the ones left behind. Remember it is always harder to be the one left behind.

This may happen to you whether it is your parents, best friend, partner, husband or wife.

Many love relationships actually end once someone starts this career. It is the rare partner that can handle the lifestyle of a reserve flight attendant. You will be gone a lot; most airlines will only give you ten to twelve days off when you're on reserve. You may not even be based where you're from, or in the area where your partner still lives. You'll be meeting so many new people it's hard for someone not to get a little jealous. You're the one that will be out having all these great new experiences, seeing new things while your partner or spouse could be feeling left behind, doing the same old thing. I don't know your current situation, but chances are if you were not in a meaningful, fulfilling relationship when you left for training, this job will not fix that. I would compare it to having a baby to save the relationship; it doesn't work. If you are in this predicament I have a feeling that you knew, at least subconsciously, that you were running away from something. Most flight attendants I asked about this subject said that they broke up for many different reasons, but used this new career as a catalyst to end the relationship. My advice is: keep the job. If this is what you really want to do, a healthy partnership will support that. This chance to be a flight attendant doesn't come easy. You were chosen among thousands of other applicants just to interview and still thousands more who were actually interviewed.

If you are in a strong relationship, you probably knew this going in. There are things you can discuss before you move into your new lifestyle:

> **Love, Trust and Support** Establish these things before you leave for training. Find out what concerns each of you have and discuss them before you leave. It is also a good idea to establish guidelines and boundaries at this point. Discuss how you will support one another when feeling vulnerable or just sad.

**Prepare and Understand** That there is going to be an adjustment to this new way of life. Set a time line to talk about what is and isn't working.

**Travel** I call this a paycation! It's true, you won't have a lot of off time or money as a new hire flight attendant, but what you will have is free hotel rooms in great cities and flight benefits for your partner or spouse. If your partner has a regular job (Monday through Friday), plan for them to be on call with you over the weekends. It will not always work out, but when it does, it will be a romantic way to re-connect on the company's dime.

**Time Together** Make the most of the time you do have together. Do special things for one another. If you are fighting on the little time you do have together, that may be the sign of a problem.

When I asked other flight attendants if they were in a relationship when they started flying here's what they said:

*Kathe:* *"I was married and to be brutally honest, this was my way out. I got on that plane and waved through the flight deck window and said to myself, there is no way in hell I'm failing stew school. I graduated and one week later asked for a divorce".*

*Brian Easley:* *"I ended one (relationship) as soon as I got the job. I knew the distance was going to be too much. Of course I was twenty two at the time so it probably wasn't going to last anyway".*

*Jim:* *"I was (in a relationship) but, it didn't work out for a whole other issue. Yet, I used it to end the relationship".*

*Monique:* *"Yes, and still married sixteen years later. Not always easy, but worth the ride. Support, understanding, patience and trust are required from both of us".*

*Cari:* *"I think whatever season of life you are in plays a role as well".*

*Bob:* *"I was a flight attendant for another airline for twenty years and I did the thing that I had always warned new people not to do. My boyfriend at the time wanted me to make more money and be home. I got the high pay, high power job. I hated it. The relationship failed and here I am a new hire flight attendant again. I have no regrets and am happy to be back flying. This is an amazing job with so much flexibility. If he or she loves you, you will find a way".*

I would say that the bottom line is this: If your relationship isn't working, it's not the job. It may have taken longer for the issues to come out and the job may be a catalyst for ending it, but if this is what you want to do and it comes down to a choice, I would choose the career. Someone who truly loves you won't make you choose.

Family and friends, while a little different, can still have trouble adjusting to your new life. Here are some tips that will help keep those who love you from feeling forgotten:

- Keep up with everyone on line. What a great tool we have today. Facebook is a great way to keep everyone up to date with your life and travels.
- Send good old fashioned postcards from all the great destinations you'll be traveling to.
- Make time for the most important people in your life.
- Most likely, you'll be flying over any and all holidays and birthdays for the next ten years. Pick alternate days that you're all available to celebrate the holidays important to you and your family.
- Skype or ichat with loved ones whenever possible.
- Have eligible "pass travel" family members meet you when you get a good layover.

It's important to take advantage of the positive things this career offers you. Those who love and support you will do that. It's an adjustment, so be patient with everyone and ask that they do the same for you.

## Love is in the Air

*I once dated a guy who lived in another state. I found it fun to jet off to visit him on my days off. Well, one time when I was supposed to finish up with a trip around 5pm the pilots informed us that scheduling had contacted them to let them know that we were all being turned. Meaning we were not finishing up with our trip upon arrival. I called my boyfriend when we landed to let him know I wasn't coming and why and since I only had the next day off I wouldn't be coming at all. Instead of getting the sympathy I was expecting he was mad! He actually had me in tears by the end of the call. After we finished our turn and headed back to base the pilots who were not based there were given hotel rooms from scheduling. Since the first officers wife was meeting him and she already had a hotel room he offered me his room. I was thrilled since that meant a nice room to myself instead of heading back to a crowded crash pad. I should mention this all happened before cell phones and internet so when my boyfriend called my crash pad the next morning and I wasn't there, he assumed the worst. He actually thought I had lied and cancelled my plans with him because someone better had come along! Needless to say that was the end of that relationship. I had too many years left on reserve to be explaining myself to anyone.*

*Then there was the cheater. I thought I would drive from my base in New York to my boyfriend's house in Massachusetts one night and surprise him by climbing into bed with him before he woke up in the morning. I was the one who got surprised when I saw a naked woman next him in bed. After my knees buckled, I tried to think quickly about what I should do; then I spotted her clothes on the floor! I grabbed them and ran out of there!*

So let's say you've now moved on from your previous relationship or you started out single and you're free to date. How exciting! You have the entire world to choose from right? Well, yes and no. I really thought guys would be excited to date me. After all, I was now a flight attendant!

What's not to love? I travel, I come with travel benefits (if I deem you worthy) and doesn't every guy (straight or gay) want to date a flight attendant? Unfortunately, this career comes with some challenges when it comes to dating. Beware of a few types:

**The Insecure Person** This person can't handle you being gone. They will drag you down! That is not why you signed up for this career. The minute a potential partner doesn't accept that scheduling changed your trip and freaks out when they can't reach you, run don't walk!

**The Cheater** This person thinks it's great that you're a flight attendant because that gives them time for Rachel, Sally and/or Rob.

**The User** They want your flight benefits. Brings a whole new meaning to friends with benefits!

It will take a very special person who can handle your new life style. Remember to put yourself first. Enjoy your new experiences and travels. Don't give up any opportunities for anyone! Remember, if someone cares about you they want to see you you fulfilled and pursuing your goals. The right person will come along. Ever hear that phrase, "absence makes the heart grow fonder?" Never settle.

# Crash Pads

*"A journey is best measured in friends, rather than miles"* TimCahill

*I loved my first crash pad. I lived there with my closest friends from training. We had a one bedroom suite with three beds out in the living room and four beds in the bedroom. It was in a very shady motel across the street from a strip joint. They had a wing for "crew" and a wing that they rented out by the hour…. Yeah, it was that kind of place. Funny that I now look back at that time fondly, but I do. The hotel provided shuttle service to almost anywhere we wanted to go, so we were able to get dropped off and take the train into New York City. We had some great times there.*

*In my next crash pad as a commuter I had a roommate that was dating someone who happened to be married… Married and famous! She met him on a flight while he sat in first class and his wife was in coach. (talk about a sign there's a problem!) The phone calls used to come in the middle of the night and keep us all up. He ended up divorced and my roommate did marry him. I say if you meet a celebrity on a flight, more power to you but, I'd make sure he or she is single. I'm a firm believer that karma, as they say, is a bitch!*

*Some things that make me look back and laugh are the calls in the middle of the night from scheduling. We didn't have cell phones when I was on reserve so the phone in the room would ring and wake everyone up. Of course we'd all be hoping it wasn't for us. There were many times you'd here profanity or someone just break down and cry. There was a male scheduler who used to refer to everyone as sweetheart. One night one of my roommates had had enough and when he called her sweetheart she said, "Hey! The only time anyone should be calling me sweetheart at 3am is if I am getting laid!" Luckily the scheduler had a sense of humor.*

One of the biggest questions you'll have to ask yourself when you find out your new domicile is, "where am I going to live?" Unless you are lucky enough to find yourself based in the city you are currently residing in, there's a good chance you will need to live in a crash pad. Money is tight when you first become a flight attendant and a crash pad is a way to live inexpensively. It's close to the airport and usually offers around the clock transportation to and from the airport.

Crash pad living is a hotel room or small apartment shared with other flight attendants and/or pilots. There are usually two types of crash pads:

**Line holders/commuters:** Line holders (those flight attendants and pilots that hold a schedule) will try to share a crash pad with other line holders because they have set schedules and are there much less often than a reserve flight attendant.

**Reserve**: This is probably where you will find yourself, at least for the first couple of years of flying. Although it can be crowded at times, because you're with other reserve flight attendants, it can also be comforting. You're all going through the same experience and you'll appreciate having others to hang around with during the slow times of year when you're on call, sitting by the phone more than you are flying.

There's not much you can do to prepare for a crash pad ahead of time. It may seem stressful to not have your plans set before heading off to training, but you most likely won't know where you are going to be based until the end of training. Silver lining? …Because your classmates will all be in the same boat, you'll be able to make plans with your new friends and figure it all out together.

Where can you find information on crash pads?

- Bulletin boards in the flight attendant crew room or training center.
- Facebook: Ask your instructors if they know of any Facebook groups for crash pads at your new airline. Facebook has become a great resource for flight attendants.
- Those flight attendants you meet on your training flights can offer a wealth of information too. Be sure to network.

What should you look for in a crash pad?

- **Affordability** If you and your classmates decide to start your own crash pad, make sure there are enough of you so the price is right. Certain hotels offer themselves out to crash pad living and they will rent to you and your classmates a room equipped with enough beds. The rate is set by the hotel and then divided amongst however many people will be sharing. They will usually set a limit to how many can share a room.
- **Hot bed vs your own bed** Although it can be cheaper to not have an assigned bed starting out, remember, on reserve you could end up spending many nights at your crash pad; you'll want to make sure you have your own bed and a little space to call your own. A hot bed is when you take whatever bed is available when you show up, much better suited for line holders who commute.
- **Transportation** You'll want to make sure there is a shuttle service to and from the airport 24 hours a day. As a "reserve", scheduling can assign you to trips anytime of the day and get you back to your base at all hours of the night. It's also a good idea to make sure the shuttle runs often enough that you're not waiting for an hour every time you get home.
- **Co-ed vs gender specific** You'll find both co-ed crash pads and female or male only crash pads. You'll have to ask yourself what you are most comfortable with. Crash pad living is a pretty intimate setting and there is usually only one bathroom. I chose to be in an all female crash pad because sometimes we would have to share the bathroom when time was of the essence. Figure out what's important to you…only you know what your comfort level is.
- **Distance to the airport** Most crash pads are close to the airport, but the closest isn't necessarily the best choice since you also want to make sure there are things for you to do close by. Maybe working out is important to you. Some crash pads that are hotels will have a workout room. I also liked having convenience stores and restaurants within walking distance to me. Find out if your crash pad offers shuttle service to places other than the airport.

- **What can I bring and keep at my crash pad?** Understandably you'll want to make your new place feel like home, but keeping in mind the space limitations, you'll want to limit the amount of personal items you keep at your crash pad. If you get a crash pad with other reserves, you should have a small corner to call your own where you can keep a couple pictures on a night stand and maybe a drawer full of your own things. If you're lucky, you'll have a little extra space to hang items other than your uniform in a closet…but this isn't always the case.

A very important thing to remember is that even though you are going to feel extremely close to your roommates and you want to trust everyone, you'll still want to protect your valuables. The only way to do that is to not leave any in your crash pad. There are always thieves unfortunately as well as people who just truly forget something is not theirs because property has become commingled.

Crash pad etiquette is also important. You may come in from a trip at 2am and be wired, but it's important to remember that your roommate(s) may be getting up for an assignment at 4am. You'll have to establish the rules and guidelines that work for you and your roommates.

Things you'll want to discuss with your roommates:

- Bathroom time limits
- Food. Will you share or label your own?
- Quiet times (after 10pm for example)
- Visitors. Are they welcome or not? (usually not)
- Cleaning duties (if you don't have a maid service)
- Sharing (deciding if you're willing to share things such as clothing)
- How much notice will be required if someone decides to move out? The rest of you will most likely be required to pay the difference if someone bails without notice.

Crash pad living can be some of the best years you'll ever have. You will never be closer to your fellow flight attendants as you are during the years you spend together on reserve. You'll go through the good, the bad and the ugly together. You'll laugh, you'll cry and you'll have the most fun you can imagine. You'll lean on each other when times are tough and scheduling is difficult, or when you think you just can't work another holiday or get another 3am wake up call. These people will be friends for life; part of your new "flying family". You'll get the most out of it if you try not to focus on the negative aspects of it, but instead, just enjoy the ride. Most likely you'll eventually get your line and you'll either transfer to a line holder crash pad or you'll move to an apartment or house. It will be bittersweet. When else in your life can you have a slumber party with adults every night you're home? It truly is a unique, incredible time in your career.

# Scheduling and Reserve

*"I travel not to go anywhere, but to go. I travel for travel's sake. The affair is to move."* Robert Louis Stevenson

*I like to compare being on reserve with being a new mother! When scheduling leaves you alone, catch up on your sleep! And, by the way now that I have experienced both I would have to say being a new mother is much harder than reserve, but that only lasts a few months! Reserve will most likely be longer.*

*One trick I used to survive reserve was to think of scheduling like my own private travel agency. I would be excited to get the call and find out where I was going next! The long layovers in great cities is what I lived for and if I had a great crew even better, but I always went out and explored on my own. I know your money is tight right now so you'll want to do some research online and find out what you can do for little money or even free in your layover city. Use Facebook and other social media outlets to connect with other flight attendants and find nearby events. I have been to museums, plays and outdoor concerts, all for free. Also, just take the day to explore on your own with your camera…you may find it to be the best way to discover a new city.*

I'm sure by now you are familiar with the term reserve. Each month, reserve flight attendants have a set amount of days that they are on call. They will be filling in for sick calls, illegal crews or wherever the need may be. Your reserve system will depend on the airline that hired you. Some airlines have straight reserve, others have a rotating system. One thing that is common with both systems is this: If you are on call, you belong to scheduling.

As a reserve flight attendant, you will be guaranteed a certain amount of hours each month. This will be somewhere between 70 and 90 a month depending on your airline. Let's say you have ten days off and you are guaranteed 80 flight hours. (flight attendants are generally paid for flight hours flown not actual hours on duty) As a reserve you may only fly 20 actual hours or what the airlines call "hard hours flown" but you will still be paid your 80 hour guarantee. You will also have months when you fly over your guarantee in which case you will be paid the 80 hours plus the extra hours flown. Again each airline has its different system so be sure to learn exactly how yours works.

Another way for flight attendants to make extra money is per diem. Your airline will pay you a certain amount of money for expenses while away from your home domicile. This will usually amount to somewhere between $1.50 and $2.50 per hour. International will be a little higher than domestic. Pay attention to the trips you are assigned. If you have any control at your airline for picking up trips, try to pick up a four day trip versus a two day trip. Your per diem will be higher and can add up to hundreds of extra (mostly tax free) dollars in your pay check; a real life saver for reserve flight attendants.

## Reserve Systems

**Straight Reserve** means you are on reserve every month until your seniority holds a line. In other words, every airline determines that they need a certain percentage of reserves to cover its operational needs. Let's say your new airline decided they need 10% of their flight attendants on reserve (this can vary from base to base and operational needs.) That means if you are on a straight reserve system you will be on reserve until you move out of that 10%. This happens when flight attendants who are senior to you transfer to a new base, retire, quit or get fired. Sometimes a big hiring spree can help, but I have found that the movement really needs to be done through attrition. Luck really comes into play here. What I mean by that is, it all depends on when you get hired. I know flight attendants who have never sat a day of reserve and I know flight attendants that have been on straight reserve for twelve or more years. This can also depend on where you are based. Some bases are more senior than others so you may only be on reserve for a year in one base, but another more senior base could be twenty years reserve. This is where commuting may come into play – we'll explore that a little later.

**Rotating Reserve** is a shared system of reserve. In the simplest of terms, it's when most (up to 90%) of the flight attendants share in some aspect of reserve, whether it's a few days a month or several months a year. Some airlines have flight attendants hold straight reserve for a certain amount of years and then start a rotation - one month on reserve, one month holding a line. Another example is when an airline may have 75% of the flight attendants sit a few days of reserve every month and the top 25% never sit reserve. There are many different systems and if your airline has a rotating system, you'll catch on pretty quickly to how it all works. There are pros and cons to both; rotating can be good for planning during the weeks you hold a line, but with a rotating system, your overall time on reserve tends to be dragged out a lot longer.

As I've mentioned, the airlines are seniority based and how they handle reserve is no different. Sitting reserve affects your ability to make more money. As a reserve, you are given a guaranteed monthly salary which can be nice when you don't fly as much as that guarantee. At the same time, you can fly a lot more as a line holder and have more hours and more per diem that may not be offered to you as a reserve flight attendant. Flying more productive trips usually comes with seniority as well, meaning more time in the air getting paid and less time on the ground not getting paid.

As stated above every airline has its own system of reserve that you will need to learn. Generally when you are on call, your scheduling department must be able to reach you. Having a cell phone gives you some freedom, but always be aware of what your minimum call out time is. Some airlines can give you as little as two hours to show at the airport. Most airlines have some flexibility with call out times and allowing you to pick up trips you might prefer. Be sure to learn all the ins and outs of your airlines reserve system.

## Be Prepared for the Call

One of the things you can do to prepare yourself is make sure your bag is packed at all times when you are on call. For example, if you are on call and decide to travel a good distance away from the airport, throw your packed bag in the trunk of your car. Before you go to bed make sure all you have to do is put your uniform on. Have everything else ready to go. It's best to have a cosmetic bag and toiletry bag that never leaves the suitcase. Remember, scheduling can call you at 2 in the afternoon or 2 in the morning. Also, make a check list of all your required items and go over it before you leave for the airport. Placing your I.D in the same spot in your roller-board after you finish a trip will prevent you from forgetting it on your next trip.

## Commuting on Reserve

Commuting is when a flight attendant or pilot lives in one city, while based in another. Commuting as a line holder is at best, challenging. You're giving up valuable time in order to fly back and forth to your job. Commuting on reserve makes this even trickier, as you will have fewer days off and little control over when your days on call begin and end. There will be times when you are stuck at your domicile after a trip due to weather delays, full flights or cancellations. And of course, there will be times when you can't get to work for the same reasons. Be sure you know your airlines policy on commuting. Some airlines have programs in place for missing flights to work. You may be given a freebie once a year or they may have a policy in place that states as long as you give yourself a certain amount of flights, you can let them know what's going on. If this is something you are thinking about doing, make sure you have a crash pad in place, hotels will bankrupt you as a reserve flight attendant.

## The Voice (scheduling)

Most likely you and scheduling will not be best friends, but you do need to figure out a way to get along because they are now a big part of your life, and will continue to be so, even after you're off reserve. Whichever airline you are at, make sure you know the rules. If you have a union, know your contract inside and out and carry it with you at all times. It also helps to know that the schedulers are just doing their job. You are a body to them - you fill a spot. If you suspect a scheduler made a mistake, and they will – they're human - never argue with them. Simply ask for their supervisor or talk with your supervisor about your concerns. Always, write down the time, date and the name of the scheduler you speak to because the airlines record your conversations….another reason not to argue and instead, handle yourself professionally!

Think of reserve as paying your dues. No matter what career you choose there's always dues to be paid. Enjoy the great trips when you get them and seize all the wonderful moments. If you find that you're burnt out, think of what the future holds. There is so much freedom in this career once you hold a line. It's worth hanging in there.

# Packing

*"I'm leaving on a jet plane don't know when I'll be back again"-John Denver*

*I was so excited when I got my invitation to training, I couldn't wait to pack. The problem was I didn't know how to pack…and that is an understatement! Luckily, I had been working in real estate for the year prior, so I had some nice suits. The problem was, I was twenty three and thought that six weeks would require my entire wardrobe…shoes and all. I packed two large suitcases, circa 1993…no wheels, a large suitcase size duffel bag, and a business travelers' garment bag. This did not include my carry-on. They actually tried to charge me for my bags on the way home from training…and back then you had to have a lot of bags for them to charge you.*

*Something I may not have mentioned yet is that I failed my first time through flight attendant training. Yes! Failed! Sent home packing! It was devastating, but luckily I was given a second chance to come back through training. Well, this time I was prepared. I had one suitcase! I knew how to pack for six weeks of training. My poor roommate, who I could not tell I had been through training already, was a mess. She finally broke down around week four…..”I just don't get it, you get hundreds on all the exams even though you don't study and you knew what to pack!” she cried! We're still friends and it's pretty funny now!*

What does one bring for four to six weeks of flight attendant training? Most airlines will require business or business-casual attire. The airline that hires you will let you know exactly what they expect. You're luggage should be an 18-22 rollaboard but before you head out to buy new luggage, find out if your new airline provides luggage at the end of training. That way you can use what you have or borrow a friends if you don't have anything that works. Trust me, we'll get to the money in a bit, but you want to make sure you save every penny at this point. If you do need to purchase new luggage, check out TheFlyingPinto.com/discounts for great deals on rollaboard suitcases. And if you must buy a suitcase, look for one that has:

- Either two wheels or four - the four wheel bags are a bit easier to push or pull
- Adjustable handle height
- Light weight
- No more than 22"
- Compartments for thing like toiletries and shoes
- Inline skating wheels
- Outside pockets for convenience

Find out what your accommodations will be. Some airlines have training centers with dorm rooms and others will be putting you up at a hotel. You need to know things like, how often you will be able to do laundry and will you be supplied with fresh toiletries when you need them? Knowing the answers to questions like this may save you luggage space and a little bit of money. Also hotels have hairdryers, so if you're staying at a hotel, this will save space in your suitcase.

The trick is to learn now how to pack efficiently. Follow these steps to pack like a pro:

## What to Pack for Training: Women

- First start with your shoes and work your way up. One dress pair, one casual; think ballet flat and sneakers. Keep the dress and casual pair the same color (probably black) and build your outfits around them.
- Five mix and match outfits for class. Meaning, stick to neutral colors like brown, black and beige. You can accessorize with scarves and jewelry to add style and color.
- Two casual outfits for the weekend
- Two or Three work out outfits
- Enough undergarments for a week

## What to Pack for Training: Men

- Three pairs of dress pants and five shirts for the classroom
- One or two pairs of jeans for the weekend.
- Two or three casual shirts for going out and relaxing in the evening.
- Two pairs of shorts, three t-shirts and one pair of sneakers for the gym
- Enough undergarments for a week
- Men need only one pair of business shoes, one casual pair, and a pair of sneakers, as mentioned above.

## Tricks to make it all Fit

You'll need a lot for these five to six weeks of training. This will be a good time and opportunity for you to learn how to get by with less while at the same time, fitting everything you need.

- Roll your clothes.
- As I said earlier pack neutral color clothing such as black or brown and add color with your accessories.
- Use space saver bags. You won't need to for a regular 2-4 day trip but, these are great for longer trips when you still only want to bring just one bag.
- Use the space inside your shoes to put things like jewelry or other small items.

## Laundry

While in training, you'll be able to do laundry either at the hotel or training center dorms. Always keep a small travel size bottle of Woolite or detergent in your suitcase. This way if you ever find yourself in a bind you can always wash your pantyhose out in the hotel sink or even your uniform. Lucky for flight attendants polyester dries fairly quickly.

## The Reserve Suitcase

Once you're online and on reserve you should keep the following packed in your suitcase at all times.

- A bathing suit
- Workout clothes
- Mix and match neutral colored clothes that can be dressed up or down and layered for temperature changes.
- A spare tooth brush
- A plastic bag for mishaps/spills on the plane or a wet bathing suit
- An extra uniform
- Spare hose (for ladies)
- Extra underwear
- Power cords (buy spares and leave them in your suitcase)
- A winter hat and gloves
- Cash (at least $20)
- A small emergency kit containing cold medicines, anti-diarrhea medication, nasal spray, bacterial wipes, antibacterial ointment and band aids.

## The Reserve Tote

The flight attendants' tote is like a passengers' carry-on bag. This is where you'll keep the items you need most. Any items that you want to have accessible to you should go in your tote. Your airline may or may not provide one for you; Travel Pro is one company that offers a nice selection of high quality totes. Here is a list of things I recommend you pack in your tote:

- Your inflight manual and all other required duty items (check with your individual airline)
- Your passport
- A flashlight
- Extra pens
- A notebook (keep records of any incidents with passengers or delays in case you need to recall a situation at a later date)
- A sweater
- A toothbrush and toothpaste
- Gum
- Granola bars, oatmeal or something non-perishable for when you are starving and don't have food available.
- Your favorite hand cream

# Required Duty Items

Required duty items are the items that the FAA (Federal Aviation Administration) requires you have with you at all times while on duty. Your airline will provide some of them for you, the rest you'll need to get on your own. Here is what the FAA requires; your airline may have some additional items:

- Current Inflight Manual
- Current ID badge
- Cabin key (on person during flight)
- Working flashlight
- Watch with a second hand

It is extremely important to have you're required duty items with you at all times. The FAA does random checks and not having your duty items can result in fines for both you and your airline. If you're inflight manual is not kept current, they can actually go back and look at all the legs you have flown since the last revision/update came out and fine you and your airline, per leg, since the last update came out!

Once you complete training, you will want to keep your suitcase packed at all times (with the exception of changing out your laundry). One trick to doing this is to buy two of everything. Whatever cosmetics and toiletries you use, have one set at home and a second set for your suitcase and tote. And Ladies, always keep extra hose in your suitcase. These tips will save you from forgetting anything and make life a little easier for you when you get that call from scheduling!

# Your Health

*"If you look like your passport photo, you're too ill to travel"* -Will Kommen

*I once turned the corner in the back of a 777 and a man coming around the corner sneezed directly in my face, it was like a bad car accident, I didn't even see it coming. I was sick as a dog a couple days later! Another time I grabbed a sick bag in the back of a seat back pocket and pushed my hand inside to open it only to feel my mistake...someone had actually used the bag for what it was intended and failed to dispose of it.*

*If you're like me you will find it hard to relax and sleep when you have an "O dark-thirty show" (as we lovingly like to call it). Your mind will be preoccupied with worry of waking up on time. I suffered from this for many years until I came up with my own solution. I set three alarms: my cell phone, the hotel wake-up call and the alarm clock the hotel provides in the room. I sleep like a baby no matter what time my "show" is. Why? Because if three alarms fail, I wasn't meant to go!*

Your first year of flying will put you into contact with more germs than you can imagine; your eating habits won't be the healthiest, your sleep schedule will be sporadic and your stress level will likely be challenged. During my first year, I suffered from a sinus infection, four viruses, pink eye and food poisoning. Most likely your airline will not have a lot of sympathy for you... after all, you are the "reserve"...you're the one here to *cover* the sick calls! The best thing you can do is be prepared and learn how to take care of yourself and your health to the best of your ability.

## Germs

Think about it this way, you will have days that you fly six legs (flights). Let's say all these flights are full...that's about 120 people per flight...120 people per flight x 6 flights equals 720 people from all different parts of the world. Not only are you contending with their germs, but also some bad hygiene. People will sometimes change diapers on tray tables, and they will sneeze without covering their mouth.

You will most likely be exposed to more germs and colds your first year of flying than ever before in your whole life. There are things you can do though, to prevent yourself from catching everything you're exposed to. If you are not already, become fanatical about hand washing. Carry anti-bacterial lotion and wipes with you. Lysol makes a great 1.5 oz spray that you can keep in your carry on, use it to spray the door handles and faucets in your hotel rooms.

## Sleep

Scheduling is going to mess with your sleep schedule. If you are someone that goes to bed at the same time every night and gets up at the same time every morning, you will probably have a difficult transition into your new lifestyle. I'm pretty sure I have no circadian rhythm. Couple that with the fact that I was young when I was on reserve and that is what made it bearable for me. There will be times when you'll get in after flying day trips for a stretch only to be told you're checking in for a red-eye turn the next day, at which time you'll come in from your red-eye to be told you need to check in at 6am the next morning. So, how do you sleep all day after your red-eye and then go back to sleep that night so you can be up in time for your early check in the next day?

You will be very tired; there isn't much you can do to control what scheduling throws at you. However, you can eat right (most of the time), exercise and sleep when the opportunity presents itself. Invest in an eye mask and ear plugs. You'll find yourself cat napping during sit time and on dead head flights….this actually will help!

There will be times when you arrive at your layover hotel early and because you got up so early you will be tempted to take a nap. Don't do it! Go exercise instead. You'll be happy you did later that night when you're not tossing and turning and can actually sleep. If you feel you must nap, set your alarm for 15 or 20 minutes before you fall into a deep sleep. Even if you don't fall asleep, 15 minutes of relaxation can help you recharge. But no more than that….trust me!

Always set your things out the night before and make sure your bag is packed with everything except what you need to get ready. This way, if and when you do get the "Oh &%#*!" call, you can throw yourself together in a hurry. Remember, you're flexible…you can spray on some dry shampoo and apply your make-up in the van if need be!

## Diet

Another challenge will be to eat right and eat regularly. You'll have long days on the plane where your only choice will be whatever you can scrape up…usually not the healthiest of choices. Refer to chapter "Food to Go" for more information on how to pack food for your trips. Invest in a good multi vitamin and eat well whenever you can.

## Exercise

Although you may not feel like exercising while adjusting to your new lifestyle because you will most likely be exhausted, I recommend you do it anyway. Luckily, you won't have to break the bank to keep fit. The hotels you stay at will have gyms that you can use free of charge and some even have deals with gyms close to the hotel. You can also go for a run or a walk, or just do some exercising in your room. What you choose to do will depend on the length of your layover and what time of day you are working. If you do go for a run, make sure to ask the front desk where the best place to run is and always let another crew member know when you go.

Some exercise equipment you can easily pack:

- Exercise bands
- Jump rope
- Empty water bottles (fill in your room to use as weights)

- Workout DVDs
- Workout apps

Some hotels are now offering in-room exercise channels. The Hyatt has in-room yoga for example. And, there are plenty of on line exercise programs to choose from too. Thank God for YouTube!

Time permitting, always try to get outside on your layovers, even if it's just by going down to wait for the van fifteen minutes early. Sometimes this is the only fresh air you will get all day! Remember, there will be times when you'll be stuck in a metal tube your entire day!

# Hotels and Layovers

*"Travel is the most private of pleasures."* Vita Sackville-West

*My family travels with me a lot. Once when my husband came with me we brought our yorkies with us. I called the hotel we stay at in San Francisco and found out the entire 12<sup>th</sup> floor was pet friendly so they told me to go ahead and bring my dogs, they would hold a room for me.*

*Hotels will usually accommodate you if you let them know ahead of time. I've been able to have a crib waiting in my room, have a family member check in ahead of me on a layover, or check out later if I had an early show. Take advantage of your benefits and have your loved ones come and enjoy your layovers.*

One of the perks of being a flight attendant is sometimes feeling like your living the life of the rich and famous by staying in great cities at nice hotels. Layovers can be as short as eight hours or as long as several days. Laying over at a nice hotel and/or in a great city is one of the best parts about being a flight attendant.

### Checking In

This is another area where seniority may come into play. It depends on your airline and crew, but tread lightly when jumping for the "sign in" sheet. Technically crews are supposed to sign in for their rooms in seniority order. My airline isn't a stickler for this domestically, but on my first international trip I learned the hard way and nearly had my head cut off by the lead flight attendant. The reason that it's such a big deal internationally is because sometimes crews have to wait for the rooms to be cleaned (I've waited up to two hours!) so yes, the most junior is the one that will wait the longest. The senior mamas and papas also know which rooms have the best views, amenities etc. As a newbie, it's best to observe and wait.

### Safety

Always (discreetly) let the lead flight attendant know what room number you're in. I say discreetly because you don't want any strangers following you to your room! Another good habit to get into is to prop your bag up against your door, keeping it open upon entering and check your entire room before locking yourself in. Always check your peep hole before opening your door and if they claim to be hotel staff and you didn't request anything, call down to the front desk to find out if they really should be there.

I find it odd that flight attendants are safety professionals, yet most I know do not wear their seat belts on the van ride to the hotel…probably the most dangerous part of our job! So buckle up!

Fires are a real threat at hotels. Make sure you know your escape routes and follow precautions. Always know where your hotel key is and take it with you if you are evacuating. If there is fire or dense smoke in the hall you may have to re-enter your room!

## Perks

Take advantage of the great amenities hotels offer. Some have free wine tastings, happy hours, pools, great workout rooms and discounts in the restaurants. You can always call ahead of time or research your hotel on line and find out what amenities are offered.

Bringing family, friends or a significant other on a trip with you is also a great perk. You'll need to learn your airlines rules for non revs joining you on a trip but, generally guests are welcome when there are seats.

## Alone Time

As a reserve flight attendant you may find your alone time has diminished quite a bit. Layovers will be a chance for you to catch up on that. Ladies, you'll find "hotel time" is great for manicures, pedicures, waxing and whatever other beauty treatments you need to catch up on. You'll also enjoy being out of your crash pad and having a TV and remote control to yourself. Hotel time is your time to pamper yourself and enjoy your time alone.

## Room Service

Room Service is generally over priced and not worth it. You can read more about room service in the chapter, "Galley Grub."

If you can afford it, don't forget to tip the maids. I usually leave a dollar. We always tip the van drivers and the maids seem to get forgotten. You can also leave goodies and/or magazines as a nice gesture if you can't part with your cash. What magazines and goodies you ask? You'll find you will suddenly have an abundance of People Magazines and extra treats to take with you from your flights.

If you do spend any money at the hotel, make sure you get a receipt showing that you paid your bill. Keep all receipts for three months in your suitcase in case there is ever a discrepancy.

## Sleep Tips

- Find something that relaxes you like a warm bath, meditation or soft music
- Drink chamomile tea
- Try melatonin (This herb works well for some and not others)
- Set three alarms so you don't have to worry about whether you'll wake up.
- Exercise (as early in the day as possible)
- Keep your hotel room on the cooler side
- Turn off the TV and try reading

I don't recommend sleep aids because you never know when scheduling will call. Remember, even on a layover there is always a possibility of a re-crew. There's nothing worse than being in a Tylenol PM fog on a fourteen hour duty day.

Enjoy the hotels, they are definitely one of the perks of the jobs! Now if only we could figure out how to get hotel points?

# Training vs Online

*"When in Rome, do as the Romans…."* Anonymous

*I was in my tenth year of flying when I got on the plane to work a trip to Madrid and couldn't figure out why this flight attendant was making snarky remarks to me during the whole pre-board process. "you're bags go in there," he said before I even had a chance to get "there." "You need to head to first class for a briefing after you check your emergency equipment," he snarled. I was thinking, "yeah whatever dude." Fast forward to the briefing and he called me out as a newbie to the lead. Ha! First of all I was senior to him and secondly the lead and I were old friends. She looked at me like, "what's he smoking?" I had just got all new luggage and turns out he assumed I was new because of my sparkling new bags and hopefully my oh so youthful looks! Lesson here, never assume and never treat anybody differently because they're new.*

You went through four to six weeks of training and you consumed a lot of information in that time. Your head is probably still spinning. One thing that happens to many new hires is they think they know better. Not about everything of course, but now that you are fresh out of training, you will see other flight attendants out "on the line" doing it their way, even though that's not the way you may have just been taught in training. Your trainers will tell you that you should be doing things the way you learned in training and not what you see out on the line. My advice is to be flexible. Don't come on the plane and start correcting line holders. You will not win any friends and in fact, you will develop a reputation for yourself. Like it or not, you just joined a system based on seniority. You will not move up by your merits, only your system seniority number. Learn from flight attendants who have been around for a while. Most are very helpful and fun to work with. Unfortunately you will come across a few bad apples, just remember they act that way to everyone, not just you. This is true in any company you decide to work for, a benefit of our job is that most trips don't last longer than four days. Imagine having to see those type of people everyday? When I was young and brand new, I have to admit, I let negative people get to me. Now, however, if I'm on a multi-day trip, I will confront anyone who makes me feel uncomfortable. I always suggest clearing the air so it's not a long, tense filled trip. You really want to avoid writing anyone up; find an alternative…your union or your companies EAP (Employee Assistance Program) for support. Of course if you find yourself in a position where you feel there could be a danger to the aircraft or people, you'll need to bring another flight attendant or pilot into the loop.

As tempting as it may be, don't rearrange the galleys to your liking. Everything you see is in the same spot on every aircraft at your airline. The next flight attendant to work your galley will not appreciate if you moved things around. Remember it's only "your" kitchen for the flight you're working. Another important thing to remember is to leave your galley as you found it. Leave it clean and in order for the next flight attendant. If you get into the habit of leaving behind a messy galley, word will get around. If you are not sure about something, ask for help. Most flight attendants are happy to have you there and are willing to help. After all, you represent their movement upward in seniority.

# Support

Most likely your airline has a private flight attendant group on Facebook. Find it and have someone add you to the group. This will be beneficial for you in so many ways. I wish Facebook was around when I started flying. My airline is hiring right now and through our page on Facebook, we've been able to hook new hires up with uniform pieces, information on crash pads, information about layovers and so much more.

If you're lucky enough to connect with a flight attendant who's been flying for a few years or longer, don't be afraid to ask him or her for their contact information. You can at least connect with them through Facebook or email. Ask them if you can call on them if you have questions and/or concerns.

Also, find out information about your airlines EAP (employee assistance program). The EAP is not just for drug and alcohol abuse. They have support for depression, sick family members and many other personal needs you may have.

If you get to the point that you're thinking about quitting, do yourself a favor and give it another six months. See how you feel then. This way, you give yourself an "out" and mentally you'll feel like there's a light at the end of the tunnel, while at the same time…a lot can change in six months.

# Flight Attendant Pet Peeves

*"I have found out that there ain't no way to find out whether you like people or hate them than to travel with them." Mark Twain*

*I hated when passengers didn't tell me what they'd like in their coffee! I'm not even sure why, but every morning flight I worked my blood pressure was rising! It never failed, I'd park the cart, say good morning something to drink? and they'd say, coffee....and go back to their paper or whatever else that was more interesting than talking to me. I'd stand there. Wait. Get mad. I tried giving them a black coffee and moving along to the next row of passengers only to be called back by a confused passenger. "Can I have sugar?" they'd shout. Then I tried adding a little flight attendant humor, "sorry, I didn't have breakfast with you this morning." I smiled. It didn't go over well. I'm thankful for my day job because I wouldn't make it at a stand up comedian. Thankfully, I hit a cross road. I realized around year five that most people were never going to tell me how they take their coffee and I let it go.*

Here are a few common flight attendant pet peeves:

- 80-90% of passengers will not tell you what they'd like in their coffee
- A lot of passengers will have head phones on when you ask them what they'd like to drink.
- Some passengers will not say "Hi", "Bye", "Please" or "Thank you".
- A few passengers will ask for water immediately upon boarding.
- At least a few passengers will board the airplane and head straight for the lav.
- Half of the passengers won't know how to open the lavatory door.

I can agree that some of these things can be annoying day in and day out, especially the head phones, but it is what it is. You can jump on the band wagon and let all these things get under your skin and even piss you off (FYI, they're never going away) or you can save yourself five years of grief and get over it now. Five years is usually the turning point when a flight attendant decides whether or not this is going to be their career. If so, they better stop allowing the little things to bother them.

**Quick Tip**: When a call light goes off, bring a cup of water with you. Especially on red eye flights - this will be what the light was for, 90% of the time.

Out on the line, as flight attendants call it you're going to come across a few "Debbie Downers". The best way to deal with them is to be happy with your choices and not let anyone bring you down with their complaining. I know some of you reading this plan to make this your career and some of you just want to fly for a few years. The career of a flight attendant is what you make of it. The reason I stuck with it through my reserve years was because I knew the freedom I would experience once I was a line holder. You will hear flight attendants say that they are only doing this for a few years and that they need something else because this job is not stimulating enough for their brain. I completely disagree with that assessment. In addition to meeting new and interesting people every time I go to work I've been able to fly around world for free, visit many amazing countries and have experiences my life would not have otherwise afforded me. I have oodles of free time and you can't put a price tag on that. If you pay your dues in this career, you will find the time to discover your passions. Go back to school if you like, take courses just because you're interested in something, start another business, have a family and of course, travel! Does that sound like a brain dead job to you? Decide early on what your goals for this career are and don't let the sour apples get to you!

# Galley Grub

*"As you walk and eat and travel, be where you are. Otherwise you will miss most of your life." –
Buddah*

*When I first started my career as a flight attendant I was not financially prepared. Senior flight attendants advised me to find dates to take me out for nice meals. I remember a guy I was dating once asked me what I did with ALL my money. My answer?..."Well, sometimes I eat." Needless to say he didn't last long.*

*Other interesting things I've seen along the way are flight attendants that will actually eat leftovers off a passengers' plate. Yah, gross...luckily not the norm. I won't touch anything off a passengers' meal; as far as I know, they could have sneezed all over it.*

*Flying with fellow reserves? Some of my best memories are setting up debriefings. A bunch of us meet up in a fellow flight attendants' room. Think food, drinks, and good times. I still plan this when I fly with friends.*

Figuring out your diet as a flight attendant can be a challenge. You won't always have a fully stocked kitchen at your disposal. Airplane food and airport food usually aren't associated with healthy eating. The joke goes: *senior mamas* look so good because of all the preservatives they eat. Luckily the airports have gotten with the times and you can find healthy and even affordable options at most airports today. Where do you begin?

## The Crew Cooler

The crew cooler is a soft sided cooler bag that has outside pockets for storing things like tea bags, condiments, and granola bars. The cooler comes in two sizes a small and a large, I recommend the larger of the two for new hire flight attendants since you will be gone often on multi-day trips. It's the perfect size bag for packing food for several days. I know you might be thinking that this will bring your bag count up to three, and good for you for paying attention! Actually, that is acceptable if you are a working crew member, as the two bag rule does not apply to you. The cooler runs about $30 to $40 US dollars and is worth every penny because you will save money not buying all your food on the road. Make sure to check out TheFlyingPinto.com/discounts for great deals on Crew Coolers.

## What to Pack in the Cooler

Flight Attendants are some of the most creative people I have ever met. I have seen everything from marathon runners to foodies provide for their needs while on the road for four days or more. My first piece of advice is to pack food that you really like. This will help you from being tempted to buy food at the airport or the hotel. The four day trip is most challenging to pack for. You'll want to make sure your cooler is packed full to keep it cold inside and be sure to eat your perishables in the first couple of days. Produce when packed well, will usually last all four days. Here are some ideas on what to pack:

**Salads**: Great to have on the road. Not only are they a healthy option but it's something you can get creative with. The trick is to keep all your ingredients separate until you are ready to eat your salad. Optional ingredients that travel well include:

- Romaine lettuce
- Tomatoes
- Cucumbers
- Hard boiled eggs
- Peppers
- Cheeses
- Carrots
- Broccoli
- Cauliflower
- Peas
- Corn
- Red onion
- Tuna packets
- Nuts
- Avocado (whole & not peeled)

Of course these are just a few ideas. If you were to go to a salad bar at most airports they will charge you per ingredient and it can get pricey. All these items will keep for your whole trip so bring enough to have at least one salad a day. Another great option is fruit. It's a nice option for an early morning get up or a snack on a long day.

- Apples
- Oranges
- Bags of mixed frozen fruit
- Freeze things like strawberries, blueberries, pineapple, and raspberries ahead of time, they'll help keep everything in your cooler, cool!

Bananas are great for the first day, but tend to make everything in your cooler smell like banana and get brown by day two.

## Keeping Food Cold

*Note: A traditional freezer pack will only last you your first day and you won't find another freezer on the road to re-freeze it. So, what can you do to keep your packed food cold?*

Smoothies are also great to make and freeze before your trip. Blend your favorite fruit and freeze, store in an empty water bottle and place in your cooler. You'll have a delicious, healthy breakfast for the first 2 days.

Refillable ice bags from a medical supply or drug store. I know a lot of flight attendants that use this method. I prefer my Ziplocs because the refillable ice bags sweat.

Packing your cooler full with some frozen food. Keeping your cooler stuffed full will help keep it cold. You can also freeze a bottle of water before your trip, it lasts for at least 24 hours sometimes longer and you'll have extra water to drink too.

Bring along some extra freezer bags and as your food dwindles you can fill the empty space with ice from the airplane and your hotel as needed. Be sure to double bag them with the seals zipped opposite each other, this will help prevent leakage. Lastly, your airline's catering may leave dry ice in the first class carts. Ask the first class flight attendant to save it for you.

## More Ideas

- A potato (sweet potatoes are great) par cooked wrapped in tin foil. You can finish baking it in the galley oven.
- If your airline has ovens in the galleys (and most do) you can marinate fish or chicken at home, freeze then pack them in your cooler and it's ready to cook in the galley oven on day two or three of your trip.
  It works great to keep your cooler cold too. Just be sure to have the galley flight attendant working first class save you a tin or if your airline doesn't have a hot meal service, bring tin foil with you.
- Great snacks include nuts and granola bars. It's a good idea to keep a couple things in your tote in case you forget your cooler. Look online for recipes to make your own.
- Peanut butter, almond butter etc. keep well and are a good energy boost.
- Instant oatmeal
- Soup in a pop top container. You can heat in the airplane oven…just remember to remove the paper label.
- Amy's frozen burritos
- Bags of mixed frozen vegetables for salad or steaming

## Vegetarians and Other Special Needs

You don't have to give up your special dietary needs just because you became a flight attendant, but you need to be aware that it will be more of a challenge for you. Even if your airline provides crew meals, there is no guarantee that you will have a vegetarian choice. Since you don't want to find yourself stuck without a meal option after a fourteen hour day, you'll want to prepare better than most. Make sure you always have a stash of non-perishables you can eat. A former flight attendant turned Raw Foodie (Girl on Raw) has a great web site and travel e-book that will provide lots of information on this topic. Her book provides recipes and ideas to make traveling as a vegetarian much easier.

## Crash Pad Chow

You and your new roommates will need to figure out how you'd like to work out the food situation, but most likely you will each buy your own. You may decide to split some staples like condiments and such. Otherwise you'll want to get labels. Just like your mom labeled your camp clothes, you'll want to label the food you keep at your crash pad. You still may come home to find something missing, but labeling what's yours should help. I recommend not buying too much at a time although this can be tricky when you're on call. The best strategy is to have a lot of non-perishables on hand. Whatever you buy fresh, should be in your "to go" plan for when you get called by scheduling for a multi-day trip.

## Gadgets to Go

There are some great inexpensive gadgets that you can carry with you. Some of these items can get expensive but if you're really into healthy eating and saving money, some are good investments. You may want some of these in your crash pad too.

- **Immersion heater**: for hot drinks or soup. I love mine for hot tea since I find using coffee makers in the hotel room make my tea taste like coffee.
- **Mini crock pot** Get creative and heat up soups and other meals on long layovers.
- **Cuisinart Smart Stick blender** Gadget for mixing smoothies.
- **Ready Set Joe Travel Mug by Melita** a great gadget if you are particular about your coffee. I have friends that swear by it. As described on Amazon: *For clean, clear, flavorful brew in about 4 minutes, the manual drip can't be beat. Near-boiling water is poured in a circular motion over grounds in a cone style filter-this creates turbulence, evenly soaking and distributing the grounds. Coffee then drips through a paper filter that traps sediment and oils.*
- **Platypus Wine Preserver** (A flight attendant must have) This gadget is meant to preserve wine once it's been opened and it also serves as a great travel bag to bring your favorite vino to enjoy on your layovers…time permitting, of course.
- **Ziplock's zip and steam bags** You will find microwaves in many hotels or your airlines crew lounge (where you may be spending many hours) Ziplock steam bags are great if you can prepare and freeze some meals ahead of time. Simply pack the frozen meal in your cooler and when ready, place ingredients in the steam bag and microwave according to directions.

## Eating at the Airport

You've got to watch yourself at the airport because a trip here and there to Starbucks can really add up fast. Of course, there will be times when you need to grab something. Here are a few guidelines for eating out at the airport:

- Set a monthly or "per trip" budget for yourself.
- Learn to like your airlines coffee; you'll save yourself a ton of money.
- Remember there are many healthy, affordable choices at most airports. You don't need to automatically run to McDonald's.
- Most airport coffee vendors will give you hot water for free when in uniform. (for the tea drinkers)
- Starbucks offers 10% off if you bring your own coffee cup.
- Your airline most likely has an employee cafeteria in your hubs. You can find affordable meals there.

Before too long, you'll know the food choices at the airports you frequent and you'll know which places have the best food options. Talk to fellow crew members and ask for their ideas regarding places to eat. They know airports like the back of their hands.

## Chicken or Beef?

It never fails, when I buy food in the airport we inevitably end up having leftovers on the plane. It will depend on your airline whether there is an option to eat the airlines food for free. Some airlines still offer crew meals - especially internationally. You will find seniority once again coming into play here, so expect to get last pick. If you work in first class, a lot of times you will find you have leftovers due to passengers turning down the meal.

Since many airlines have started selling meals and snacks on board you could buy the airline food…but don't. Bring your food. If you find yourself hungry and food-less, wait until the onboard service is over; most airlines allow their employees to eat anything that is perishable and will be thrown away otherwise. Eating the airplane food should only be done on occasion because it is filled with preservatives and sodium. Don't worry if you feast on junk for a few months, most new hires do. Your body will reject the idea after a while and crave some real nutrition. It doesn't take long to get sick of the airplane chow.

And, last but, definitely not least: BYOB or BYOW (wine) or whatever your hearts' desire. You are allowed to carry your own spirits on board, just be sure to follow your airlines guidelines for bottle to throttle. You'll need at least eight hours, and some airlines require more.

# Hotel Dining

When on your layovers you will have a choice….eat in, from your cooler, order room service or go out to dinner. Of course everything will depend on the location of your hotel, the amount of time you will be there and what your budget will allow. I recommend spending less money at the airport and saving that money for when you have a great crew and a great layover. There will probably be times when you can't afford to go out and remember, we've all been there. But when you can…do.

Room service is mostly overrated. You will spend a lot more money than the price displayed on the menu. Look for the fine print. Most hotels add a service fee, gratuity (not sure what the difference is) and tax. All this can add up to almost double the bill. Your airline probably worked out a discount so be sure to let the hotel know who you are when ordering. Another way to spend less is to order off the children's menu or get a bowl of soup. The soup is usually a meal in itself served with bread.

You can save a bundle (all the fees) by ordering from the hotel restaurant and going down to pick it up yourself. You'll still get your discount and you'll avoid the fees.

There are hotels that have microwaves and/or refrigerators in the room. You'll start to know which have them and thus be able to plan your trips better. You can always call ahead to find out too. All hotels do have refrigerators and offer them at a daily charge. Flight attendants are the most clever people I know and I recently flew with a reserve flight attendant on a tight budget who knew how to get her fridge for free. If you have medication that needs to be refrigerated (and you do, don't you?) the hotel is required to provide one for you. Once in your room call the front desk and request your fridge for your medications.

# International Travel

If you find yourself leaving the country, there are some things you need to consider. Find out what the exchange rate is before you leave the United States. Yes, there are apps for that. Also, you'll want to find out ahead of time what food is permitted into your destination and what food is permitted back into the US.

Don't try to sneak anything in! If your caught, at the very least you will find yourself detained and at worst, fines and possible job loss. Don't think you're exempt if you're a domestic flight attendant either. If your airline flies to Mexico and Canada there's a good chance these destinations are out of the domestic base.

# TSA and Airport Security

As a flight attendant you are exempt from the 3.4 oz rule and can bring as much liquid as you need within reason. I usually pack a full large crew size cooler and have a bottle filled with water, no problem. Be careful, however, if you are a commuting flight attendant or out of uniform, TSA will usually hold you to regular passenger guidelines then.

# International versus Domestic

"Two roads diverged in a wood I took the one less traveled by, and that has made all the difference." -Robert Frost

*When I started flying the first thing I did was put my transfer in for international! If I was going to sit reserve I may as well be going to Paris and Milan! I had to wait four years before I ended up in an international base, but my very first overnight was in London. For someone who had never been to Europe that was ok with me! I was called to sit at the airport on call and the scheduler added, "bring your passport." I think that was the most excited I ever was to sit ready alert! A few of my classmates were sitting there as well and we were so excited with the possibilities. The phone rang and two of us were called up to a 747 headed to London. This was better than Christmas and my birthday combined! Unfortunately when we arrived at the aircraft they only needed one of us. I backed out and went back downstairs. The scheduler promised to get me somewhere and she delivered. There was a second flight to London and I was on it! When I got to my hotel room in London I called my friend from the first London flight in her room. She was so out of it that she asked why I was calling her. I said, "we're in London!" She said, "we are???"*

If your airline has international flying and the bases are separate from the domestic flying you'll have the opportunity to decide what kind of flying you'd like to do. Of course you'll have to put in a request for what base you'd like and if you don't get your choice right out of training, you will probably be able to put a transfer on file. I had my transfer on file for the international base the entire time I was a reserve flight attendant and never did get my transfer while on reserve. Once I was a line holder I pulled my transfer and waited a few years until I would be able to hold a line internationally before putting it back in. I did finally make it there and hands down it was the best time of my career. There are many "pros" to flying internationally and if you are young and single, it's a must!

Becoming a flight attendant is an education in itself. You will learn so much about yourself, people and the world around you. Take full advantage of everything. Even if you only fly domestically, you will meet people from all different cultures and backgrounds. Having an open mind is essential for succeeding in your new career as a flight attendant. Always try to see things from the passengers' perspective; it's the only way to truly learn how to excel at customer service.

Whether flying domestically or internationally, try to see and do everything that is available to you. Do a little research online if you know you'll be in a cool city for twenty or more hours. Make your plans and go see what is of interest to you. You don't need money to walk around and take pictures. All cities offer freebies; certain days major museums are free, summers offer outdoor concerts and markets. Do you love to paint or draw? Take advantage of the new landscape. There are so many things do and there is no excuse, not even money (or lack thereof) for not making the most of your travels.

There is no reason to ever be bored as a flight attendant. Maybe you had a "real" job before this…If not, ask your friends with real jobs how much time they have to read books, take an online class, visit new cities or just day dream. Even if you have a family at home, this career gives you a little extra YOU time.

## Pros of an international base

- An education that you can't get in any classroom.
- A chance to see the world on the airlines dime
- Best Christmas shopping ever!
- Late check ins (mostly)
- Great sightseeing/photo ops
- Did I mention the shopping?
- Longer flights (The advantage to long flights is fewer boardings, which is generally the hardest part of the day.)
- A chance to learn a foreign language

## Pros of staying in a domestic base

- Closer to home if you have young children
- A chance to see your own country if you haven't traveled a lot yet
- Great layovers in great cities
- Less expensive (your airline will probably give you a little bit of an "over ride" on your per diem if you're based internationally)

Fatigue can be more of an issue if you fly internationally and/or red eyes. Scheduling may assign you some day flights and some red eye flights all in the same week. Fatigue will be a big part of your life until you are off reserve.

If you do choose to fly international you'll have to figure out what sort of sleep cycle works for you. Talk to other flight attendants and find out what works for them. I found sleeping for two to three hours tops upon arrival in a foreign city worked best for me. It will be extremely difficult to get up after a nap, but I found that if I did that I had enough energy to sight see and get through my day and was still tired enough to sleep that night.

You won't be able to avoid jet lag, but there are a few things you can do to try to acclimate to the different times.

- Be in the best shape you can. Make your health a priority with this job and find the time to exercise.

- Once on your flight, set your watch to the time zone you will be arriving in.

- Plan to "be" on the time zone you will be arriving in. Once on your flight try to sleep if it is night time at your arrival destination. Set an alarm to wake when it is morning at your arrival city.

- Once you arrive, if you must take a nap, limit yourself to 1-3 hours. This is difficult and you'll want to sleep longer, (In fact you may want to shoot yourself, rather than get up) but if you do you will have trouble going to sleep on time in your new time zone.

- Try melatonin. It worked for me, but I had crazy dreams so I don't like it. I know many people that love it.

- Have a night cap! No, not the alcoholic version. As tempting as that may be, your sleep will be interrupted enough without adding alcohol. Stick with a night time tea, like chamomile.

- Go to bed at the time of night you usually go to bed, in your new time zone. You may still feel groggy the next day and/or wake through the night, but this is the best way to get enough sleep for the trip back the next morning.

# Stand By

*"A good traveler has no fixed plans, and is not intent on arriving."* ~Lao Tzu

*Once I started flying internationally my mom came on many trips with me. It was a great time in our lives. She'd meet me in New York and we'd jet off to Dublin, London, Lisbon or Rome. It always seemed to work out too. My mom has the best luck and non revs in first class more than anyone I know! She came on a Christmas trip with me to Rome and we were there for a few days due to a lesser holiday schedule. We had an amazing crew and spent Christmas Eve at a family owned Italian restaurant celebrating. I'm pretty sure she ended up kissing our first officer good night, but I don't want to start any rumors! And, then came Birmingham, England. It was a great trip. We layover in the cutest little town in the world, Stratford Upon Avon, but her non rev luck was about to run out. The return flight looked wide open when we made our plans and it still looked wide open the day before departure and then another airline cancelled a flight. Arghhhhhhh! I was in the midst of boarding the flight as door greeter when the gate agent asked me to come out on the jet way. There was my mom holding back the tears. "I'm fine." she stated. And, she was. Her nerves got the best of her as this had never happened before. The gate agent even offered to let her stay at her house! In the end she got a hotel room and made it out the next day. Just goes to show, you always need to know your back up plan. Especially if pass riders are with you while you are working. Many times you won't even get to talk to them before they shut the door without them.*

Free travel is probably one of the main reasons you chose to be a flight attendant and that is great. Take full advantage of your new benefits. Stand by or "non- reving" is a term we use in the airline industry for non revenue travel. You can now fly free or close to it (depending on your airline). If only you could afford to get hotel rooms! Now is the time to make good friends in great places. Just like everything else, seniority plays a role with stand by travel. Most likely at your airline, you'll board according to your year and month of hire. Next will generally be family members and then other "pass" riders such as friend passes and other airlines.

Each airline will have their own pass travel system. Most likely your family members, including spouse, partner, children and parents will be included. They will be known as your "pass riders". Be careful who you choose to let use your benefits. Make sure they are responsible. Your pass riders, in a way, have your job in their hands. Make sure they know to always be respectful and professional. Never barter or sell pass privileges, you will most likely lose your job for that.

Find out what the written dress code is for your airline and make sure you and your pass riders adhere to it.

Non-rev etiquette is very important. Find out what the written rules are for your airline because if these rules are not followed by you and your pass riders, not only is there a chance you won't get on the plane, but you could lose your pass privileges or worse…your job!

Here are some standard rules that apply to every airline:

- Be polite, say please and thank you. It's a simple gesture that makes flight attendants and gate agents very happy.

- Be patient, the gate agents are working very hard to get the flight out on time, they know you're there.
- Be humble and accept the seat you are given graciously.
- Check your bag when asked to check it (make sure you keep any medications you may need or valuables)
- Never expect anything. Depending on the airline and the rules they follow, some flight attendants may offer you things like a glass of wine or a bottle of water, but don't ever expect it.
- Don't bring attention to the fact that you are traveling on a company pass.
- Don't expect to sit in first class, but if your airline allows non revs in first class, dress appropriately just in case.
- Drink responsibly. Your behavior reflects your company.
- If a flight attendant asks you to move to another seat to accommodate another passenger, please do so.
- Follow the rules just like every other passenger has to; never feel you are above them.
- Most important of all? Make sure your pass riders know all the rules too! If they have an issue with an employee, have them contact you and let you deal with it. If they are confrontational, even if they are in the right, they could cost you your passes or your job.

Use your own resources to figure out how to visit the places you'd like to visit inexpensively. Some ideas for places to stay:

- Friends
- Youth hostels
- Couch surfing (there are many reputable sites for this type of travel, just make sure you use common sense and keep yourself safe)
- Hotel discounts. Your airline will have discounts at certain hotel chains, find out which ones)
- Discount sites like Priceline.com that let you set your own price.
- Sites like www.airbnb.com that rent apartments, houses and even rooms that are very affordable.

There are also all kinds of discount sites for airline employees and hotel rates that your co-workers will be able to fill you in on. I've also added some sites in the resource section.

You'll have your good days and bad days non-revving. Generally speaking, summers, holidays and spring break can be difficult times to get on a flight.

Another perk to being a flight attendant is you will probably have "jump seat" benefits. This means since you are qualified to sit on the jump seat that you can catch a ride on the jump seat if there are no other seats on the plane. Your airline may also have agreements with other airlines to be able to ride their jump seats, too.

You'll also want to find out the agreements your airline has with other airlines for you and your pass riders. You will be able to buy discounted fares; these are usually known as ID90s, meaning you get 90% off of the full fare price of any particular flight. Check with your airlines travel policies to find out information about this and how to purchase tickets from other airlines.

Your airline will have many resources for you that will give you discounts on not only hotels and other airlines, but also rental cars, shipping companies, resorts, cruises and more.

All in all, I believe that stand by travel is a great perk, but always have a plan B. Even when flights look great, things can go wrong. Flights cancel and even if it's not your flight that cancels, that cancellation can mean your flight has now filled up. If you're traveling for vacation, it doesn't hurt to have a couple places in mind. If your flight to Rome fills up, go to Paris! Traveling off season helps too.

You just have to be flexible, which I know you are!

# Wisdom Stew

"Flight Attendants are the most creative, innovative people I know." -Sara Keagle

I want to leave you with what I refer to as "Stew Wisdom." When you're at 35,000 and you're missing something (like five first class pasta bowls) you'll have to figure it out. Flight Attendants are amazing when it comes to problems like this. Not only are we able to "make do" with what we have, but sometimes we can even make it better. There's no "Seven- Eleven" or corner store in the sky; many flight attendants have been through tough mergers, cut backs, furloughs and more. Flight attendants are like kids that don't have a lot of toys and are able to become the most creative, innovative people you know. So here is some quick, random advice from the people who know best…my colleagues:

## Your Moola ($$$$)

*Alex*: As soon as you can, have the maximum allowed percentage coming out of your check and into your 401K and NEVER borrow against it.

*Heather*: Whenever you get a raise, bump up your 401k contributions so you never notice the pinch.

*Deborah*:
1. Live beneath your means and SAVE from the very first check.
2. Per diem is for layovers, not your car payment, so eat well and enjoy yourself.

*Amy*: Hire a tax professional that specializes in airline crew taxes. It is worth the money as they will itemize your per diem.

*Kenneth*: Invest in an extra battery for your cell phone and computer when you can.

## Love at 35,000 feet

*Pamela*: Don't sleep with the pilots…seriously, that about covers it.

*Laura*: If he does not look good at the first drink, those beer goggles will have you fooled by the third and he will become your knight in shining armor by drink number four. This is a trap. Don't EVER drink them 'pretty'.

*James:* They are (passengers and pilots) always cuter when they are sitting down.

*Cari:* Don't quit this job for a boyfriend or girlfriend.

*Jennifer:* Don't date the jealous type—even if they say they trust you, but are "just jealous of your job".

*Michelle:* Be open. You never know when love is in the air.

# The Practical

***Alex:*** *Make a very detailed "To Pack" Checklist and keep a copy above your suitcase at home, and another one inside the suitcase.*

***Kelly****: Wear comfortable shoes.*

***Patricia****:*
*1. If you can't find the blow dryer in your hotel room, check in the bathroom drawers and it may also be in a bag inside the closet. If not, call the front desk.*
*2. If you get into your room and cannot get any of the lights, tv etc. to work, check to make sure that you do not have to place your key card into a slot right inside the door to activate. I think this mostly applies overseas.*
*3. If you can't get out of your room because you only have two doors and one is to the bathroom, and the other has a sign on the handle saying "Do not Enter" you need more help than I can give here.*

***Moya:*** *That short looking sink in the bathroom next to your toilet is NO sink, wrong end.*

***Katia:*** *Remember what you said you were willing to do when you applied for this job. Remain flexible, keep a positive attitude and refine your skills when it comes to dealing with unpleasant people, be it customers or fellow crew. Your life will be a lot easier because of it. Don't let others change you.*

***Carol:*** *Always put your passport BACK in your "stowed position" as soon as you clear the Immigration Hall so that you don't lose it in the rush to get to the employee bus or you next gate.*

***Cady:*** *Take vitamins…. you are nothing without your health.*

***Cari:*** *It's okay to wear the same pants / skirt/ blazer for the whole trip. Please do bring clean shirts though.*

***Cathy:***
*1. Be downstairs at least 5 minutes before van time.*
*2. Take advantage of the free breakfast if the hotel offers it.*
*3. If you're going out alone, let someone know or leave a note in your room.*
*4. Do not collect air samples!*

***Cari:*** *Wear nice pajamas to bed. You never know when the fire alarm might require you to leave your room.*

***Carol:*** *When you get to your hotel room & take your ID off, put it in your shoes. Chances are that no matter how foggy your brain is the next morning, you won't show up for the van without your shoes! (Or your ID, now!) That's also good advice for any small things like watches &*

jewelry that you take off at Security. You won't leave it behind unless you walk off without your shoes!

***Christoph:***
1. Always be early; fashionably late is only for parties.
2. Have a place for each required duty item where you can always find them.
3. Smile like you mean it, the world is bigger than most problems and it's all available to you.

***Debbie***:
1. If you're not five minutes early for the van then your late.
2. No one knows how to open the bathroom door, help them out - don't yell at them.
3. The pilots are part of your crew, treat them with respect.

***Jennifer***: A smile can change a persons' day.

***Alicia***: When you can't get your drapes to close all the way to keep the sun out, use that clothes hanger with the pant clips on it.

## The Fun Stuff

***Jennifer:*** Keep a journal. Keep a journal. Keep a journal. You think you won't forget but you will. You and your family will be glad you wrote it down!

***Christy***: Have plenty of (safe) sex.

***Brenda***: If at all possible, fly with a friend - it makes your layovers that much better! On reserve, I know you have little control, so be friendly and make lots of new friends. In this industry, your friends will often become your support and will feel like family.

***Carol:*** Start a log book of all the fun, kooky, exciting and unexpected things that happen to you on your flights. As you progress thru your career, you'll be able to recall people & places when you tell those funny stories in the bar over a glass of wine with your crew. Some of those memories you will cherish for the rest of your career!

***Angelica***:
1. Take lots of pictures.
2. Try new foods and learn about new cultures.
3. Enjoy the ride; this is an easy job…There is no need to get into arguments… the people in that metal tube will leave your life in just a few hours. Remember, we came here because, as opposed to other jobs, when we say "Good Bye…Buh Bye!", we really mean it!

***Moya***: Never just stay in your hotel room. You may never see that layover again. You can sleep when you're dead.

# Resources

Please visit my site www.theflyingpinto.com. I am always discovering new ideas for air travel and constantly updating & adding discounts.

www.facebook.com/JetlaggedComic. The amazingly funny cartoons in this book are by flight attendant and cartoonist Kelly Kincaid. You can buy her cool products at, http://www.zazzle.com/jetlaggedcomic

www.travelproluggageoutlet.com Use code: theflyingpinto15 for 15% off your entire order. The discount applies to the entire web site, but to access the "airline personnel" section enter your airlines two letter code (UA, AA, DL for example) and your employee number.

www.hoseanna.com My favorite resource for hosiery. Get 20% off your entire order with code: theflyingpinto15

www.3floz.com Use the link here for 15% off your total order of great TSA friendly toiletries. Great gift ideas for friends and family.

www.smartplanethome.com Filtered water bottles, lunch boxes and more. Use code: theflyingpinto15 for 15% off your total order.

Diamondveneer.com: Add some bling to your uniform! Save 50% with code: GROUP

www.dunejewelrydesign.com: My favorite jewelry line! Capture those beach memories by having a special piece made with sand from your favorite beach vacation or honeymoon! Save 15% off your total order with code: theflyingpinto15

EZPerdiem.com: Don't forget to have your per diem calculated! You're leaving money on the table if you don't. Save 10% with code: PINTO

Accessdenied.com wallets and passport holders keep your debit and credit card numbers safe from thieves! Save 15% with code: theflyingpinto15

GirlonRaw.com: flight attendant turned raw foodie has amazing travel tips for raw foodies and vegetarians.

Vegan on the Fly: A great resource for vegan flight attendants

Sara Keagle is a Flight Attendant for a major U.S. Airline, creator of [The Flying Pinto Blog](#) and [Huffington Post Blogger](#). Through her blog The Flying Pinto she shares her experiences and offers you a glimpse behind the galley curtain. She also created and co-hosts a popular podcast, The Crew Lounge, offering listeners a unique look into the life and career of a flight attendant. Sara has appeared on many morning shows including Great Day Houston, Charlotte Today, FOX News in Houston, Smart Family, Sonoran Living, and Daytime a nationally syndicated talk show.

Sara's travel advice was featured in the October 2012 issue of Oprah's "O Magazine" in the "101 Best Pieces of Advice-Ever!" She has freelanced for publications such as The Wall Street Journal's Speak Easy Blog, Jaunted.com and UPGRD.com, and serves as a resource of various national media outlets including Oprah.com, USA Today, The Wall Street Journal, MSNBC, The New York Times, Budget Travel, Trip Base, The Washington Post and Parenting Magazine just to name a few.

Kelly Kincaid is a flight attendant by day and cartoonist by night. In 2012 she launched [Jetlagged Comic](#), a strip about airline crews, their passengers and the wacky world of air travel. [Jetlagged Comic](#) grows daily in popularity among flight crews around the world. Her works has been published online and in print. She lives in Seattle, WA with her boyfriend and their surrogate cat, Miss Meow.

CPSIA information can be obtained
at www.ICGtesting.com
Printed in the USA
BVHW010224070521
606749BV00012B/412